Dying...

Surviving..

Thriving.

Written by: Hailey Barker

"The mess you work so hard to hide, may be just what someone else needs to see today, to know they aren't alone." -Jennifer Thompson

My desire in sharing this book with you is to "let you in" on my story. I hope you find common ground, from the idea of either thriving or surviving... two categories that, ultimately, every situation be labeled. I want to share my everyday hot messes so maybe yours won't feel "as messy" as they would if you were journeying through them alone.

However, I've found, sometimes I have to discover things on my own. When someone says something to me very directly like, "calm down," "relax" or even something more encouraging like "breathe in and out" I struggle to initially commit and reap those benefits, simply because someone is directing me to do it. I like to make decisions on my own, for myself, which is surprising, because I am also the type of person whose headache miraculously disappears the second my tongue touches the Tylenol pill. Life is a mind game.

My Peloton was gifted to me from my husband for Christmas. It is p.e.r.f.e.c.t for my lifestyle, it fulfills so many gaps, enabling me to live my best life. I loathe the instructors, but for some unknown reason when someone else is telling me "this is going to be the best day," (as they often do) I am not always convinced right off the bat.

I have never been into yoga, I love the idea of it, but I can only take so many deep breaths, I am distracted by what is going on around me, and I am a visual learner so I HAVE to keep one eye on the instructor or I can't comprehend her directions without the model. It's all silly to me, I can't focus the way you are supposed to, and I feel like an idiot. Maybe the negative attachment to yoga originally stemmed from the last time I attempted to attend a true class (which was probably ten-ish years ago). I got into a car accident on the way. The other car reported I was trying to make a left turn from the right lane on a one way, double lane street through downtown. There is no way I would ever try to do that, but I also have no idea if I did try to do that, because I don't actually remember. So when the insurance agent asked me a million questions, all I could say was, I THINK I was in the left lane, and apparently "I think" isn't solid enough to get the damages covered by the other party, who I remember, very vividly, was very unkind and grouchy. I even got out to make sure they were okay and they refused to roll the window down and talk to me. I was in a big Trailblazer at the time and they were in this little beat up silver car. Me, trying to talk to them through the window, them refusing to roll down the window or make eye contact, made for a very awkward situation. So I got back into my car and called my husband who was field training to be a police officer (he was really proud to be summoned to the scene for his wife). Anyway, I was late for the yoga class after that and certainly not relaxed, which is really a prerequisite.

I find I have to develop feelings and attitudes on my own and I have to be the one that decides if it's going to be a good day. I have to be the facilitator of the deep breaths if that's what I need to calm down. I can't be told. I can accomplish this through songs, because no one is talking directly to me and I can make the discovery on my own through connecting with the lyrics. Songs are powerful to me, especially as I am a Literacy Specialist, so engaging with text to make meaning is my specialty.

So as much as I want to offer advice to you through these recent experiences, I understand you will take or leave each piece. If anything, hopefully you can relate, or be glad you can't relate (but smile at my antics). In life, you can either laugh or cry in response to intense situations. It wasn't until the last couple years I developed enough emotional intelligence to choose to laugh, when I have enough self control to choose of course...

To Begin

Sometimes I think we underestimate the power of taking a deep breath. First, it is free. Second, rarely do we stop our bodies long enough to take one of those breaths where you flare your nostrils really wide to devour as much air through them as humanly possible. The kind of breath you feel in your belly and hold, only to then slowly let out. Those kind...always make me feel better. One hundred percent of the time, they make me feel lighter, despite the situation. The silly part is, I usually forget it's an option or available.

I read once in *Superlife* by Darin Olien, about the idea of surface breathing. The idea that we don't ever actually give our lungs the proper amount of oxygen they crave, but instead do these little breaths that keep us surviving but not thriving.

Knowing I have to work for 30 years before I can claim full retirement, my husband has always said he can see me making it to year 29, deciding I'm not happy, and following my heart instead of sticking it out one more year for the money. I am not self driven by money, I am self driven by the thought of only getting one life to live. The thought is also terrifying because it means we only get one shot. One shot at being each one of my kids' mom, one shot at being 32 years old, one shot at careers, vacations, and houses. I can feel Cody Johnson's lyrics to *"Til you Can't"* in my bones (if you haven't heard it, look it up!) and I want to make sure I never fall short of the moment I will never get back.

So although I do desperately want to lose weight and tone up, because I only have one shot at life, it doesn't matter to me that I just made myself six strips of bacon at 10 pm at night because that was my craving. And not turkey bacon, because that is disgusting, I'm talking real bacon. You'll find out later why I have such strong feelings against turkey.

I think of life in comparison to water. Water can be the sound of waves humbling every thought and bone in your body, or it can be the water bottle that busted in the bottom your bag, that you knew nothing about for 24 hours, ruining a $200 graduate textbook, a $350 Rapid Automatized Naming Assessment Kit Manual, and the textbook my boss/principal (that I idolize) let you borrow from a workshop she did out in California over ten years ago (which, I did manage to find and reorder for $72, wasn't planning on telling her so unless she reads my book, will hopefully never know). Too much of anything, (even fruit) is unhealthy and life is about finding that balance, walking that fine line of not overdoing it but also not shortchanging it.

One of my worst fears is letting the moment pass me by, but what about when it's a moment I don't want to experience? I thrive in feeling emotions, and I know the negative ones help me to appreciate the positive ones even more. But in order to thrive in this life, we do sometimes have to detach ourselves from draining and depleting emotions. The subconscious power to live through a moment, yet not be negatively emotionally triggered is pretty powerful. It takes a lot of self discipline. This helps me before I get upset with my kids. This also helps me not take things so personally all the time. It helps me stay focused and not get wrapped up in drama. I detach, stay positive, and move on, not holding any grievances.

I understand the way people treat you is 99% of the time a reflection of their own inner struggles. Instead of thinking less of them, I empathize with them, and I absolutely do not take it personally anymore. Before I am that person reacting from inner struggles, I try to stop. I remind myself of how badly at one point in the past I wanted something that I now have. Sometimes we do get "too comfortable" and start taking things for granted. For example, the day I am frustrated at work, I listen back to the voicemail, I can't seem to erase, from central office offering me the job. I remember how excited I was to be picked, to get the opportunity to live out my dream job. When my own children are driving me nuts, I remember my life dream, my sole purpose for living was to become a mom. I think about how others struggle with infertility and I go back to the skin-to-skin moments after they arrived into the world for the very first time. And when I feel like my house is just something I possess, that is always messy, I relive that first walk thru, thinking it was out of our reach because of the price. I try to take myself back to the exact moment I stepped into my very first classroom, the pregnancy test that read positive, and the letter I wrote to the original homeowner when we placed our offer on the house, that included my vision of where I saw the Christmas tree placed.

I know I am happiest when I am feeling confident. I try to always get myself there. I can remember in high school, during a psychology class, our teacher, who was very well liked, asked everyone as a warm up to anonymously write about something that motivates us. He collected all the written responses and read them to the class aloud. When mine was read out loud, it stated, "When I come to school in an outfit that I love, I feel motivated for the day." And immediately one of my friends, also like the hottest guy in the school, says to everyone, "YEP, THAT IS HAILEY'S." I couldn't even deny it so I dropped my head out of acceptance. But that is what motivates me, when I can find confidence in who I am. I am at my mental worst when I feel like I am falling short, which is equivalent in my mind to failing, and by failing I mean I could have done something better. If I didn't do my best as a mom, wife, friend, worker, or as just myself, I would be letting myself down. I like to wake up and dress up. I want my nails polished, and make up pretty, and I shave my legs every single day, because in my mind it means I am putting forth as much effort as I can.

You can be bogged down by the thought of always being able to do better. Because in reality, we can always do better. As exhausting as it sounds, if you think back to anything you have ever done in your life, you could have done some part of it better (although maybe not healthy...), you could have put more time into it, had more patience with the person, woke up earlier, worked out a little longer, ate a little healthier, devoted more attention to your kids. These thoughts keep me powering through, but also cause me to shut down. I try to settle myself by accepting my efforts, being grateful for the energy devoted, and satisfaction from making it to the finish line.

I can remember laying on my back, on my mother's kitchen floor as a child, stating how bored I was, thinking it was the most miserable feeling. I don't say this because my life really was boring as a child, I was constantly entertained and involved in so many things, but I can clearly remember numerous times laying right there on the cold tile floor as my mom made dinner or wrote out bills telling her "how bored" I was feeling.

It is ironic how I would pay big money to go back to that state of mind. Actually having the freedom to lay on the kitchen floor, saying how I truly felt, and being bored. I can't remember the last time I even got close to what it is like to feel boredom. But although I dream of a bored state of mind, deep down I know boredom for me could be dangerous. If I got more than about 60 minutes of it, I would probably let my feelings of being unproductive get in the way of enjoying that calm. We often desire what we don't have, just to obtain what was missing, then long for what we had back. Life is funny that way. My husband doesn't understand why I sometimes straighten my perm. That kind of explains it.

In a way, another one of my biggest fears is being bored. I don't ever want to be seen as boring. I can not pack the same lunch each day, repeat outfits (I don't buy new clothes, I just keep mixing and matching them. I still have clothes from high school I rotate around), nor can I wear my hair the same way two days in a row. When I get the opportunity to meet up with a friend for lunch or a drink, I secretly make a bulleted list of stories I could tell them because I am afraid of having nothing to talk about. This can be exhausting. In a life that craves a little bit of boredom, I certainly don't ever even give myself an ounce of a chance to experience that. Sometimes I don't know how to not be my own worst enemy.

Light the Candle

No idea where I ever heard this, but I can remember the saying, "Light the candle, even when no one is coming over." This is so powerful because it makes us self reflect on why we light a candle in the first place. Do we do it for ourselves, or do we do it for others? I think for years I did it for others. I wanted others to think my house smelled good.

I used to think my friend in college was insane for going to the movies by herself. I couldn't understand how she would feel comfortable going out in public by herself. Wouldn't everyone think she had no friends?

I used to waitress at TGIFriday's and I would see many people come out to eat by themselves. I wondered, *how could they sit there, and not be paranoid that people weren't looking at them*? It wasn't until the last couple years of my life that I started lighting the candle when no one was coming over. I've learned to be okay with just me.

I also started going for car rides by myself, just through the surrounding towns. When I am alone I do my best thinking. I can bring myself out of dark holes and reflect on all the good in my life when I am by myself. It is often hard for me to see all I have when I am not alone. It is a strange thing, but reality for me. I cherish my time alone now, and although rare, so rare that all three of my kids know what a women's menstrual cycle is because they are literally always in the bathroom with me. (My one year old daughter even tried to pull a tampon string before and grabbed a fresh one from the cabinet, opened it, and attempted to stick it in her bellybutton...) She stands outside the shower holding my towel, waiting for me to be finished, so I can take it from her. What is supposed to be a two minute alone-time shower turns into a duo affair. Sometimes it takes alone time to get recharged. I look at people in public by themselves with such a different perspective then I used to. They may be recharging.

I recently discovered "12 Hours of Crackling Fire Place" on YouTube. I swear I can feel the heat from it some nights. There have been a few nights my husband came up to bed and found me passed out in front of "the fire." These last couple years I have worked hard on building my bank of simple pleasures. I hope you are able to find time to spend with just yourself, be your own best friend, and feel the heat from the digital fireplace.

Pay for Peace

I bought a brand new Jeep Compass from a dealership out of town. It came with two years of free oil changes, but since this dealership was so far away, they hooked me up with one closer to my house. So 3,000 miles later I was pumped to use the credit. Oil changes are expensive these days!

Well, worst experience of my life. Anything that possibly could have gone wrong did. I was without a car for as long as it was there and they kept the thing for more than 24 hours! They even forgot to put the oil cap back on when they were finished. I said never again would I return. They were rude and unkind. I emailed a complaint and was accidentally included on the e-mail thread going back and forth amongst coworkers. To say the least, there was no compassion or remorse.

I would rather pay fifty bucks to take it to the Lube Center. Those workers, girls and guys, are some of the nicest people I have ever met in my life. I leave there every time with a smile on my face because of their hospitality. They are also genuinely happy people as they sing and dance as they work. I will pay every time. I will forgo my free oil change, to escape from that headache, every single time.

I think this idea is applicable to life in general. There are times, we have to "pay" for peace. The quality of what comes to us free, isn't always worth it, just because it is free. We have to work for what we want, we have to keep looking elsewhere when whatever is right in front of us, is junk. My two year old's obsession with Matilda, specifically Matilda **the Musical** on Netflix, often rings in my mind. If Matilda, a five year old that totally raised herself, comes up with a solution for life not being fair, we can too.

Sometimes the nicest thing I can do for myself is let my kids buy lunch at the school cafeteria. I am so hard on myself about packing the perfect lunch for them, when in all reality, they just want to buy anyway. Pay for peace, let them buy lunch, and subtract one thing from the nightly chores.

We have to cling to places and people that make us feel worthy and whole. I have friends that I have met along the way. They never doubt whether or not I am a good person. They see what I offer the world, not what I can't. They do a better job at being non-judgemental than even I can pull off. Even if I don't reach out to them in my time of self doubt, I think of them, because it is their voices that build me up and remind me that I am enough. More than enough, really.

Everyone needs people that believe in them. They need outside voices that turn into those inner positive voices. Oftentimes we believe what we are told, so surround yourself with people that are building you up. As a teacher, I have always been good at finding the best in students, because if I don't believe in them, they won't believe in themselves. And if I don't find the admirable characteristics they bring to the table, it is going to be a long year for the both of us. I never struggle to find the positive in people. When I was a classroom teacher, I used to give awards to every single student. Basically "made up" awards, awards that magnified their unique characteristics and attributes. I have never had so much parental admiration. When we find the best in others, we will reap the internal benefits. Sometimes we have to work hard to find what's good in others, when it isn't blatantly obvious. But if we put the time in, it will be worth it in the end.

Sometimes, all three of my kids are crying at the same time, which isn't often, but it does happen. For example, one time when my kids were six, four, and one, we were getting ready for my son's flag football practice. I had just gotten home from work. The kids were basically thrown at me as my husband hightailed it to his work.

To help you understand, my youngest constantly wants to be held, so there have been times I was literally nursing her while brushing one of the boys' teeth. The multitasking struggle is real with this kid. She is along for every ride and physically part of everything I am doing at all times (which I did long for and wouldn't change for the world).

So my six year old opened the door and it crashed over my four year old's foot, so he started crying. Moments later my four year old bit down on his tongue while he was eating and it was bleeding, so after he pulled himself together from the door disaster, he again started crying. Then moments later I realize (the same son with an infatuation of touching pans and burners, who is forever asking if they are hot and then planning his next move based off the response to the question, meaning if it is hot, of course, he doesn't touch it, but if it isn't he has to touch it; a strange quirk that I thought was a phase, but has now lasted at least a year) this time however was different, because he didn't ask, and he just slammed his hand down on a burner that I had forgotten to immediately turn off after moving a pan away. Excruciating pain and blood curdling screams followed. His hand had the burner ring all the way from his palm to his fingertips. Second degree, at least, burns. In response to this, I had to put my one year old down, so now she was crying, because she wants to be held. My six year old was also crying because he thought we were going to be late to his flag football practice, and while he was waiting for me to walk out the door he tied his cleat strings together and was unable to walk. Somehow the bathroom door gets locked from the inside and he also has to use the bathroom but can't get in.

Cool. These moments are rare, but they happen, and when they do, my mind goes to a happy place, making it possible for me to be the calm my children need me to be instead of the storm or the trainwreck that I am walking into.

Have you ever been to Disney World's Animal Kingdom? Because I had never seen Avatar before I got onto the Navi Journey Boat Ride, but that Navi Journey is my happy place. That majestic forest is my inner peace. I can visualize the trees lighting and fireflies glowing. I can hear the water rushing and the sounds of nature. This place has a permanent setting in my mind. It helps me navigate life and see the light when I am feeling surrounded by darkness. I was a little disappointed when I came back home and watched the movie to see the destruction that an outsider can do to such a magical place, but I am reminded that nature can always be reborn. Like the truffula trees in The Lorax that had been gone for oh so long.

Have you read *Where the Crawdads Sing?* Sometimes the place I wander to mentally is the marsh where Kya grew up (and don't base your knowledge of the marsh off the film, it has to come strictly from the book). In my mind, I lay in the sand and listen to the tide and gulls. I can be still enough to analyze a feather, like the one Tate gives Kya.

I hope you have a place you can go to when your physical or mental space is closing in, because you are your only way out. And if you have the means, sometimes it is worth just paying for peace. Value the people that build you up, keep their presence in your mind alive. Figure out how to transfer your "happy place" memories into your long term memory file folders so you can reference them immediately upon request. And remember, "doing your best" does not mean doing something until you are sick.

Middle Child

It can't be easy being the middle child. Maybe I should have cut my sister a little more slack growing up. For my son, it's no joke going from being the "baby" to the middle child. And although my husband is not in agreement with me as I abide by my son's extreme wishes to lay with him each night as he goes to sleep, I still do. Because he is only going to be little for so long. He is five and the only five year old I know that gets treated as royalty, getting his back rubbed as he falls asleep. (I too got my back rubbed every night as my mom watched the news. I would fall asleep on the couch and my dad would carry me in each night. I think to this day, that is why I find the news boring, because its use when I was a child was strictly to bore me to sleep.) Anyway, my son says he's "scared" and can't possibly fall asleep without me in there. If he takes a nap during the day, I'm screwed. The kid is up all night. Well, not all night, but that is what it feels like. Then I complain because it is taking forever for him to fall asleep, and I am thinking of a million things I need to do, and then my husband is irritated because he says I shouldn't be in there baby-ing him anyway. Once he is asleep I am able to sneak out and he lasts most of the night in his own bed. Except for last night when he comes running over about 3 am stating his rabbit got out. So he snuggles up all comfy cozy in my bed and I go on a rabbit hunt at 3 am. The rabbit had ventured into my oldest son's room and was getting his rabbit all stirred up. Both of them are named basically the same thing, Striker, and the escapee, Strike, because my middle son likes to do everything my oldest does. (My middle son is also super indecisive and a few months later renamed him "Shotgun" and I never agreed to it, because I don't like guns. Then he proceeded to tell everyone at his school his rabbit's "new" name, as I held him for "Blessing of the Animals" at my son's Catholic school. That was embarrassing, as I stood there feeling like an unfit parent.) Both rabbits think they are in trouble as I am scolding them. At 3 am in the morning. You can't just grab them either, especially the one on the loose, because they take off. Once you get them, they will let you hold them, but they don't like being picked up. So the chase lasted for about 20 minutes. At 3 am in the morning.

My middle son is a lot like his rabbit. Wild. Kind. Funny. We were up at his great grandma's today and his only exposure to a pool table is in her basement. It's a classy one, kept in the most meticulous condition, cemented to the floor. Nothing modern, very 1970's (I only know that time frame from That 70's Show). He asks me to play a round with him.

He takes the triangle thing, fills all the balls within. He gently takes it off and is left with a pyramid of balls. I don't think he ever really heard the rules before, so I try to talk him through it, as much as he is willing to hear of course. He has no idea the scratch ball is what is supposed to drive you around the table. After I explain its role, he lines it up with the triangle shape of balls. He hits that sucker as hard as he can, missing every single ball in the formation, beelining it straight for a hole. I smile and he smiles. My smile comes from laughing at him. His smile comes from more pride than I have ever seen beaming from someone. He says to me, "I am pretty good."

Tonight he tells me I tied his karate belt so tight it started to push pee out of him when he sat down to stretch at his lesson.

I am often bothered by the idea that my parents know a side of me that I don't know. I don't remember, obviously, what I was like as a little kid. Pictures weren't as abundant back then (my kids will know what they ate for breakfast, lunch, and dinner every single day of their existence since birth). I hope I was a good kid, my mom says I was... it is actually what haunts me when my kids are acting up. I'd love to go back and be a fly on the wall during my upbringing. I want to see how my parents handled difficult situations, and how they interacted with each other and us. I found a diary entry I wrote once that said, "Mom and Dad are in a bad mood today," and that makes me laugh so hard because my interpretation of a bad mood was probably very similar to my middle son's interpretation of that of a liar. He said, "You always lie to me mom, you say we don't have money to buy toys when I know we really do." Interpretation of situations can always be so dynamic. Hopefully as I continue to raise my kids, they will learn empathy, so they can always try and consider everyone's perspective.

Validation

If I asked you to think of someone right now that you felt completely comfortable around, who would come to mind? What makes them feel "comfortable"? To me, it is someone that makes it possible to let your guard down all the time, to not feel as if you are walking so awkwardly on eggshells. It's someone who sees only the good in you and never questions your character. And someone that seems to think higher of you then you often think of yourself. It's someone that thinks you are funny when you aren't even trying to be, and smart, and kind.

There aren't many people that will come to mind because these people are rare and hard to come by. Your identified person(s) can't be someone that is only comfortable to you some of the time, either. They have to play that positive role in your life all of the time, because that is who they are innately.

The people that come to my mind have presented themselves throughout my life at such different times and places. They are on my side and make me feel heard. They are "my people," the people I naturally gravitate towards and they make me want to be a better person. They inspire me and motivate me for basic daily life. FIND THESE PEOPLE and do not let them go. And if they can't physically surround you, let their voices be the voices in your head.

Sometimes, we need validation in who we are as a person. There is nothing wrong with that because we are human. We don't need to spend our time around those that make us question who we are, or make us never feel good enough, causing us to lose our words, disabling us from thinking straight when corresponding with them. I also know a lot of those people. There will always be more of those people.

People that do not make us feel comfortable are often insecure, which doesn't always rub off well on others. Insecurity sometimes leads to jealousy. It creates a negative filter and whatever the situation may be, it is looked at by the jealous person through a very pessimistic lens.

I find there are two instances I can use an auditory strategy to either "get by" or enhance my quality of life. When I am surrounded by situations or people that make me feel uncomfortable, I have found searching for environmental sounds is life (or moment) changing. For example, if we can focus our mind enough to find the rattling of the leaves, the air condition that just kicked on, or the birds chirping, we can slow down long enough to recenter ourselves. If we are flustered, we can not hear the obvious sounds, so we must train ourselves to listen.

I have found, on the few accounts, that I go grocery shopping alone (Food Lion to be exact, a former high school sales associate here, that then handed my job down to my sister, who then passed her job down to my brother), I find myself mulling over the music being played throughout the store. I wonder why I only notice it when I am shopping alone. The volume is always the same, it is my mind that is different. When I am shopping with my kids, my attention is so focused on my kids, asking one to stop laying on the store floor, asking another to stop playing tag, opening every single item in the cart for them to start eating (with the bribery of getting it only if one remains sitting in the cart) etc. I could never hear that music, until I trained my mind to listen, when listening does not come naturally.

I think about the last time I was in an uncomfortable situation simply because the person I was around did not see in me what "my people" see in me for whatever reason. I was able to listen to the air conditioner that turned on almost as a saving grace to keep my mind busy. I thought about how cold it would feel if I were right up against it and how amazing it would feel coming in from a hot summer day. I thought about how I used to put my face right smack in front of the car vent after jumping into a car that had been sitting in the sun baking all day as a kid. I forgot about the anxiety because it was being stomped on by my new control over my mindset.

And while the chapter is titled Validation, I am reminded of my own sons who I know thrive too off validation. Even when people don't acknowledge the praise, they internalize it. It is a shot of dopamine for the soul. There are many elementary school students that will not respond back when an adult in the building says, "Good Morning." Before I had kids of my own, I too may have mistaken that for a behavior of choice. But just like kids are juggling a lot, so are adults. When we assume everyone is trying their best, our approach to others can be a lot more supportive than judgemental. When in doubt, give the praise out. And find people that support you. Start listening. We don't live in an underpopulated or silent world, so the possibilities are endless.

YOU'RE tired?

Do you feel how that "YOU'RE" is accented when you read it to yourself? Now read the title out loud and you can really feel how the tone of your voice changes for the word "you're" stressing a particular intended meaning. Do you ever hear someone else complain about something and in the back of your mind think how much easier they have it than you, regarding whatever they are complaining about? For instance, when your friend, with no kids of their own, says she is tired, and you have a 6 year old, 4 year old, and 1 year old.

But in a way, everyone is drowning. And although my water may be 7 feet and your complaining coworkers' water may only be 1 foot (meaning, they just need to freaking stand up...), at the end of the day, drowning is drowning.

Everyone's perception is their reality and it isn't fair to compare. Comparing gets us in a lot of trouble. We compare our hard times to other people's filtered times posted on social media. We create unrealistic expectations for ourselves based on stories we hear that may have been sugar coated by others. (I never sugar coat. I will never make my life sound better than it is, because why? Why do that to someone else who may be hanging on by a thread?) (I will literally tell you when I am wearing one of those weighted cami's that make you look way skinnier than you truly are with no hesitations.) I genuinely appreciate the raw stories shared by others. For example, there's the time when I realized at my son's lacrosse practice, I had left my car in drive but the entire time I thought it was in park. I had gotten out and left it for 90 minutes. I told my friend this as we were packing up the kids and she told me she did that the other day, only with her kids still in the car. Those are "my people," the ones that don't hold back their flaws in hopes that no one will see. They own them and laugh and do better next time.

But back to the idea of accenting words. I was recently trained in a literacy language intervention program. Accenting syllables is a real thing and if you can memorize the rules that go along with it, for example, "accents are usually placed on the first syllable if the root has two syllables," it can help you become a better reader. If you were to call your dog Rover back into the house, you would say ROver, not RoVER. The part of the word that comes out stressed, or a little stronger, louder, and requires your mouth to be opened a little wider, is accented. Tone of voice is huge when cultivating meaning. You could read the same sentence three different ways, stressing a different word in the sentence, changing the sentence's meaning each time without actually changing any of the words. For example, "I don't want to go to the PARK." Meaning, I want to go somewhere, but not to the park. "I don't WANT to go to the park." Meaning, I don't "want" to, but I will. "I DON'T want to go to the park." Meaning, I will not go to the park, because I don't want to.

So when I hear two separate friends say the same sentence, but stress different words, I find myself pondering whose side I am on. I am also guilty of being around someone and then wanting to adapt to their style. (After watching *Inventing Anna* on Netflix, I just wanted to be so fancy. But while reading *Where the Crawdads Sing*, I yearned for a remote, minimalist, and simple lifestyle). Almost the exact same sentence was used by two different friends, portraying two different meanings, ironically said within the same week, consisted of something like this, "I never imagined my life would be where it is now." Except the two versions went as follows:

"I NEVER imagined my life, as it is now, 15 years ago." (Meaning, she was disgusted being a parent of three running around like a chicken with her head cut off, having no time for herself.)

"I never IMAGINED my life WHERE IT IS now 15 years ago." (Meaning, this is what life is all about... tag teaming the evening with her husband, one person taking one child to gymnastics, while she takes the other one to karate. This is truly her living out her dreams.)

Both were separate conversations for me and I could relate to both sides. I have never been so exhausted in my life versus living my dream, to the point where, heaven forbid, if I died, I could honestly say I would go knowing my life up until this point has played out exactly how I dreamed, despite the fact that I am tired. I never wanted to be anything more than a mother. If you asked at age ten what I wanted to be when I grew up, I would have told you, a mom. I wanted to be a mom for Halloween one year. And when my then highschool sweetheart (now husband) was dragging his feet proposing to me our senior year of college, I almost died, because I knew in order to be a mom, I needed to be a wife, and I needed to be a wife yesterday. I have always been obsessed with the idea of taking care of things. LIFE, SIMS, and Rollercoaster Tycoon were my favorite board game and video/computer games as a child because they mimic life itself. It didn't matter if it was an animal, or a plant, I loved taking care of things (and still do). Many people in my life have randomly told me I would make a killer Hospice nurse (maybe killer isn't the best choice of words there...). I spent many hours volunteering in our local nursing homes and animal shelters in my high school and college years. When I taught highschool, I took my Independent Living class to Genesis Healthcare on a field trip because I wanted them to see life through my eyes, through brightening someone else's day, through volunteering. I dreamed of taking my own biological kids to nursing homes to visit the elderly. Unfortunately, COVID has closed many of those doors.

When I was doing my student teaching in college, one of my students brought me a dozen roses one time. I remember going to the nursing home that evening to visit a few residents I had befriended. I gave out the roses. I thought, either I can make myself happy holding onto 12 roses, or I could go pass them out making 12 people happy, instead of just me. I like taking care of living things and I love making people happy.

We can make each other happy if we stop comparing our lives to others, realize everyone's perception is their reality, follow our heart, give of ourselves, and pay attention to the words that are accented or stressed by others (and even our own sometimes).

Let it Go

Seriously, anything causing you negative energy, let it go. Most things that upset us, we are not able to change or control so let them go and do it immediately.

Like the day I didn't make it through the parking deck barrier gate in time (not sure if it malfunctioned or I was just too slow...) and the thing came slashing down onto the hood of my car... or the time I sent a canteen thermos container with coleslaw in it for my sons snack and the pressure built up inside so intensely that I was unable to twist it off to clean it. My husband was out of town that week and mother-in-law even tried to get the lid off unsuccessfully. So I let the thing sit on the counter until I could come up with a different plan, which never happened. As I put my one year old to sleep one night we heard a combustion that was so loud I thought our house was under attack. Having no idea what caused the sound, and not daring to mess with an almost-sleeping-baby, I came downstairs the next morning to find a hole in our ceiling's drywall surrounded by 3 feet in diameter of coleslaw caked to the ceiling.

There is absolutely nothing that crying is going to do to fix a situation 99% of the time. We might as well pick up the pieces and begin putting the puzzle back together, whatever that may entail.

There is a boy in my son's PreK 4 (all four year olds) class that talks to him constantly about his broken home. This is all very new information to my son. My husband and I were high school sweethearts. Well, he was mine, we started dating the first year after he had graduated, but then we went to the same college together and haven't broken up a day since-- almost one time, but it never happened. Anyway, the little boy told my son his parents aren't together anymore and they fight in front of him all the time. There are apparently numerous "bad words" said between his parents to each other. I guess my son was coming from a place of empathy, either wanting to make him feel better, or possibly not knowing what else to say, so he shared this story with me that he volunteered as his response to the little boy, "My dad chokes my mom. Ya know, how dad chokes you sometimes, Mom?" No. Oh my God.

He will jokingly put me in a headlock that I absolutely can't stand because I do not like wrestling around (despite the fact that I have three males living in this house, plus a male dog). My husband thinks it is funny and so do the boys as I try to squirm out or use my only defense mechanism, which is to pinch. My husband is a police officer and he drops the boys off at school in the morning, entering the building in his police uniform. If the teachers overheard my son's attempt at relating to the little boy, they would probably think we are living a facade in public and have this domestic violence secret at home. My purpose for sharing this story is to condition the idea that there are so many circumstances that are just out of our control, but are so not worth losing sleep over. The old me would have lost a LOT of sleep over small stories like this that now just provide a good laugh.

It is also important to consider others' intentions. This gives us the opportunity to let things go. I look back on my life and all the social conflict I was ever involved in with friends and boyfriends and had I considered the other person's intentions, it would have saved a lot of really close relationships from falling apart. I would have been able to move forward with the relationships, but because I got so stuck in the action, moment, or response, I went through many best friends in my highschool and college years.

"You can't let your daughter eat from the corn cob, that isn't good for her (while she is happy as a clam gnawing away)." "You shouldn't have let her get on that ride, she is too little (as she is literally on it...)" "How dare you take your eyes off her when you are at home?" "Babies aren't that dirty, why would you use that much shampoo?" The list goes on and on. I want to do everything perfectly and I want everyone to think I do everything perfectly so I struggled for a long time with comments like these thrown my way. This used to eat me alive. But instead, I now consider the intentions behind the comments. I think about the fact that maybe the person that is saying them lost a child, saw a child suffer, or is thinking about a storyline they watched in a movie or read in a book that ended poorly for the child. I think about the hurt that must come along with that pain. You would see that devastating scenario in every passing child. Comments are coming from a place of deep love and care and shouldn't be taken so personally all the time, by me.

I know their intentions are not to label me a bad parent, and although they can feel overwhelming and sometimes suffocating, they are coming from a positive place. And because I am able to now consider intentions first, I am able to immediately let things go, even when it is hard.

Gratitude Journal

As we already know there are two perspectives to every situation. We can see the glass as half empty, or we can see the glass as half full. Sometimes there are two opposing sides and both sides are actually valid. My husband is really good at seeing the glass half full, which is irritating sometimes when I am looking at it, thinking about its emptiness. But throughout our years together, I believe he has rubbed off on me quite a bit. Something that has really helped train my brain to see the positive side of things is keeping a gratitude journal. The idea actually stemmed first from doing one at night with my son. I always worry my kids are turning into entitled human beings that haven't been given the opportunities needed to truly appreciate things and not take them for granted. Which, isn't a horrible thing, ideally it means they, knock on wood, have been provided a very fortunate lifestyle. Starting this journal with my son at night helped him to reflect on all the things he was grateful for that took place during that day. It is also fun to read back through past entries with him. We really do have a lot to be thankful for, but if we don't make it a point to talk about it and highlight the details, sometimes we miss the importance and significance of them.

My brain does better when it is focused and on a mission. I started a gratitude journal probably a year or so ago. My brain is constantly searching for things I can put in that journal throughout the day. My brain's mission is to "find the good, find the good." I am looking at life through a glass half full because I want to identify areas of my day to be grateful for. If I am experiencing a pretty lousy moment, I can try and figure out what I learned from that situation that overall enhances my quality of life. We can always win in situations... either it naturally goes our way, or we end up learning a deep lesson in some aspect of life.

I wake up in the morning thinking about what I can put in my journal and I go to sleep at night reflecting on my day to identify what I can put in my journal. Sometimes I write specifically about people, while other times I write about things, moments, and feelings. I do get in my head sometimes the thought of a journal outliving me and that is why I have never kept a diary with my deepest darkest secrets (I don't really have any anyway, but I guess I am referencing any negative thoughts). I would never want someone to read it and feel hurt by it. That is even stressful with my gratitude journal because I wouldn't want someone to be hurt that they WEREN'T in it. Two of my favorite scripts *13 Reason's Why* (which my high schoolers, I was teaching at the time, got me into) and *Verity*, written by Colleen Hoover, have storylines based around something that was produced by a person that outlived that person. At least if all my notes are positive, I don't have to worry so much.

I also find myself in moments that I am afraid I will forget. Moments I will want to be taken back to sometime in the future because they were that great. We all know life can be a cluster, but if we have something to fall back on when times get tough, we will make it out okay. Without the bad we can't appreciate the good. And the more we think about the good, the more good there seems to be.

Air Fryer, House Cleaner, Audio Book, and Nail Dip

All my friends have a house cleaner. I always felt with three kids and a husband that has worked nights for the last 12 years, *we more than anyone* needed a house cleaner. We have never stressed picking up after yourself to our kids. We say, "it's time to cleanup" when we are at other's houses and my kids just look at us like a deer in headlights, unsure of how to proceed, most likely thinking, "we don't clean up our own toys, why would we attempt someone else's?" They have never had a chore chart. I am not proud of this, we are just so busy, and I have always been slightly a control freak and feel like it is easier to just do it myself. Plus they put a lot of energy in the activities they do and part of me feels bad expecting them at age five and seven to do work around the house. And let's be honest, the house blows up within seconds. I never had chores when I was younger and maybe that is why I feel so caught off guard at the amount of work it takes to keep your house functioning and sanitary (God bless my own mother).

But in my mind, as a mom, the mom should be able to keep the house clean. A good mom cleans the house. The kids deserve to live in a clean space. Although I have a full time job, I will clean after they go to sleep at night. Well, that's ALWAYS the plan, but... That always sounds like a good idea, but then remember I devote at least an hour and a half to bedtime (which requires me laying down pretending I am asleep, too, in a dark room...), I then need to pack lunches and snacks for the next day, complete work for the National Boards, complete work for the Administrative Certificate I am working toward, clean the rabbit cages, water the plants, and the list goes on and on. One of the best decisions I have ever made, throughout my entire life, is to get a house cleaner.

It went against everything I always thought. I thought I couldn't trust someone we barely knew in my house without us there. I thought getting a house cleaner would be a sign of failure on my behalf. I thought I would look inadequate. (My mom is going to find out we have a housecleaner when she reads this book because I can't bring myself to admit it.) Get a housecleaner.

She only comes once every other week, but to know she is going to take care of the bathrooms, the steps, and mopping the kitchen floor, has brought so much fresh air and pure happiness to my mental state. I was going to feel like a failure either way, because otherwise the bathroom wasn't going to get cleaned, the steps were not going to get vacuumed, and the kitchen wasn't going to get mopped, despite my intentions, without the house cleaner. There is not enough time. I don't clean when the kids are with me because I want to be mentally present with them (you should see how paranoid I am about being on my phone in front of them--and our phones are needed for so many different reasons. I am so afraid they will remember me as an absent parent, because I was always looking at my phone instead of them, so I try very hard to minimize my phone time in front of them. The AppleWatch has been such an important accessory to me, because I can quickly read and respond to necessary text messages etc.). I decided I would rather feel like a failure because I had someone else do it, than feel like a failure for not getting it done at all.

We have the nicest house cleaner I have ever met. She is also the only house cleaner I have ever met, however, she has to be the nicest and most personable and least judgemental one ever. I don't even want her cleaning up the pee on our bathroom floor (I have literally seen my boys peeing, then turn while peeing, and see pee go all over the wall and floor) because she is so sweet. I trust her with everything. I thought no one was trustworthy. She has taught me to be more trusting. Walking inside the door on days she was there, knowing someone is at my house cleaning while I am at work, makes me think what a fool I was for not devoting $35 dollars an hour to such an uplifting service.

The day she came to see the house, I knew if that didn't scare her away, nothing would. In order for me to give her my attention, I had to let the kids do their thing, which meant they were straight dumping toy bins and walking away from them. Amidst that, my husband coached baseball and I was the team mom, so we had all the jerseys for players to stop by the house and pick-up sporadically. Everytime someone pulled up, the dog went nuts, and our conversation had to be paused.

The first day she came, she wanted to do an initial deep clean. She was there at 7:30 am, was still there when my husband drove by at lunch time, and then STILL there when he got home that day at 3:30. She is a blessing to my family in more ways than she will ever understand. We obviously needed that deep clean.

So if the house cleaner makes life a little easier, you better get the air fryer, too. IF YOU DO NOT HAVE AN AIR FRYER, GO GET ONE. They make everything taste so much better. I had always wanted one, and even got my dad one for Christmas. I really wanted it for myself, but didn't want to spend the money, so I came to terms with buying it for someone else instead. He doesn't understand the value of it. He will use it for chicken wings, but it is worth so much more than chicken wings. I have made salmon, rotisserie chicken, all kinds of fresh vegetables, GRILLED CHEESE, and the list could go on and on. It is quick. It is healthy, and there is minimal clean up. Every mom deserves an air fryer. Grateful to my mother-in-law who gifted us this one for my 32nd birthday. (It comes very close to the snow cone machine I got from my husband for my 30th birthday. It is like the real deal ice shaver. Someone used to sell snow cones out of their van when I was pregnant with my second son. I followed her posts on social media, showing up wherever she was scheduled. Following my pregnancy cravings that were strictly for snow cones, were for this soft shaved ice. And when she wasn't where she was proclaimed to be, I was not happy. Distraught.) I am always so psyched when materialistic things make our lives a little easier, a little better, but holding something with such high regards, also makes the fall that much harder.

I had to take my one year old daughter to the emergency room one morning at 6 a.m. for a bout of croup that scared me. She had been okay throughout the night, but the croup got worse as soon as she was up, and that is the opposite of how it's supposed to play out. We always treat it with breathing the steam from the heated shower and then go directly into the freezer for deep breaths (if you have a baby and need to do this, put one of their toys in the freezer and have them dig for it--it forces them to become one with the freezer. A friend told me about this a few years ago and it was one of those-- why didn't I think of that, moments). The Pediatrics Emergency Room experience was amazing-- we were in and out, surrounded the whole time by extra friendly employees from registration to the doctors (maybe 6 am is the magic time to go...). We got her all squared away with a dose of steroid and we were on our way home. She was in great spirits and I knew her day was just going to consist of watching her obsession, "TILDA" (Matilda the Musical) with her Gram. So I went into work an hour and a half late. Within being at work for twenty minutes, my phone went off. I was helping the sixth graders dissect pig hearts at my school, which is quite humorous because I remember very clearly being one of two students that sat out during biology in high school when we dissected a pig. The school wanted extra hands on deck, so there I was when my phone went off from my son's school. I was getting a phone call from the nurse stating my oldest son was in the health room because he didn't feel well, but he was going to try and stick it out. She wanted me to be aware just in case I was called again to come get him in the near future. So I was relieved that I didn't have to leave early from work since I had already arrived late. I returned to the dissection.

About twenty minutes later my phone rang again from my son's school. My middle son was now at the nurse. He had collided heads with another student and she was telling me she did not believe it was a concussion. He was being sent back to class with an ice pack. Returning back into the room once again, I thought to myself, please no more issues, I just want everyone to be thriving, wherever they are. As soon as my prayer was written, I looked down at my phone, which had an incoming picture from my mother-in-law who was staying with my daughter. There appeared a picture of our beloved air fryer, with the cords cut right in half by scissors. Apparently there had been a recall on the product, the one we had used every single day for probably the last six months or so, with a note on it that my MIL wrote stating "Rest In Peace."

In order to get another one, one that wouldn't accidentally burn down the house, you had to prove you dismantled your other one. So within a few short hours, not only were all three of my children in jeopardy at some point, but now the air fryer was right there with them. They were all three able to walk away, however, my air fryer was not.

If you have the house cleaner, and the air fryer, you must add the audio books to your life. As I mentioned above, I am responsible for cleaning the rabbit cages. I didn't think this would be weighing so heavily on my shoulders when we got the two cute Holland Lops, but I also had no idea they poop up to 200 nuggets a day. I cannot in my heart make my sons clean that. The cages are in their rooms too, and any air freshener is lethal to rabbits. Their sense of smell is so strong, air fresheners kill rabbits in minutes. Since the bunnies' cages are in their rooms, I can't have them smelling badly and if I can't use an air freshener, I better get cleaning! Maybe you don't have a rabbit, but I bet you can think of many tasks you do have that take away from life's happiness, such as doing the dishes, folding laundry, or having a long car ride to work.

I was always so against audio books, because as a Literacy Specialist, I know the value of holding the book in my hands and the high dopamine levels I get everytime I turn a page. But if you are a busy mom, you don't have time to stop, drop, and read. You never stop and you never drop (well, when you do...it is lights OUT), therefore you don't get a chance to read. So now, you can drive-and-read or clean-and-read or workout-and "read" or listen. You can let your worries and anxieties go, jumping into the life of someone else. You can be that fly on the wall that sees a great story unfold with no responsibilities of your own. Mason Cooley's famous quote, "Reading is a place you can go when you have to stay here," was always one of my favorite quotes for the classroom. I remember my mom helping me set up my very first classroom, asking me if I thought that saying was "too depressing." Yes, you are stuck here right now, but your mind can be absolutely anywhere. AND WHO DOESN'T WANT TO GO ANYWHERE THEY CHOOSE without having to pack? No, that quote isn't depressing...it's freeing! If you aren't sure where to start, look into Audible through Amazon, or your public library, where you could get audio books for free.

And to complete my list of materialistic necessities, if you are someone that likes their nails done and is not available to go sit at a nail salon for hours or interested in dropping hundreds of dollars, look into powder dipping your own nails at home. You can do it at night, after kids go to bed, because it is instantly hardened, there is no paint that needs drying, that gets instantly messed up after getting into your bed, and it lasts for about two weeks at a time. It also looks SO GOOD!

It only takes about ten minutes to apply. Our hands are a part of everything we do and they are always being seen by their owner and others. Dipping your own nails is not even comparable, at its least, to the cost of a salon, looks fabulous, dries instantly, and applies quickly. Hire a house cleaner you trust, buy the air fryer, listen to the audio book, and buy the dip... because you deserve it.

Resort to Robot Mode

"It's their life, I get to live in it" is a saying that makes me feel better because it detaches the emotion and entitlement that would lead me to feel disappointed. It's a saying that I made up, that helps, when within just two seconds, two defeating seconds, a whole mindset can plummet. For example, when I was sleeping, in my bed, that is so comfortable, all of a sudden my one year old reaches for her chocolate milk, which is sitting on the headboard right above my pillow, accidentally drops it right on my face, startling me so I snap upward, but as I jump up, she is standing on my hair, that was on the pillow, and my head gets ricocheted back down. See if it were "my life only" I wouldn't be happy about what just went down, because that isn't supposed to happen first thing in the morning. But because I can resort to my quote referring to living in my daughter's life, it doesn't seem like a big deal. Almost something comical instead. Consider a third person perspective. Seeing that in action would have made anyone laugh, except for the person it was happening to.

In my opinion, being a "good mom" is not always doing what is best for me, but first what is best for them. Even if it is something as little as agreeing to get the same flavor of Rita's Ice simply because your son says he wants to be twins, even though I don't really like the flavor he chose. It is about getting it anyway because it makes him happy. It's about ordering a Number One meal from Burger King and being okay with trading my Whopper with my son's four piece chicken nuggets (which now are only three) from his kid's meal because he "wished he got the burger," and within minutes permanently handing off your medium iced tea to your other son that ordered a milkshake instead of a drink (because he said he was thirsty). Or, when I am sitting at my son's gymnastics practice and my one year old daughter is strapped in a stroller that she doesn't want to be in, especially not when she is surrounded by all kinds of fun looking equipment, and practice lasts a full 60 minutes and it has only been 15 and all the snacks have been consumed. The stress that comes along with knowing the importance of being seen by my son taking the gymnastics lessons or else he will literally fall out, while trying to control an unhappy one year old that doesn't want to be contained, while simultaneously helping my six year old with homework, is real. It is out of love and compassion that I do these things, like simultaneously serve three children at the same time. And although an odd thought to find comfort in being just a "part" of someone else's life, opposed to leading my own, the idea of something being out of my control releases so much pressure I put on myself. When I can reason with decisions being made, I can sleep better at night. When moments aren't going my way, it is easier to be a supporting actor opposed to the lead actress in a play. The weight of a "mess up" doesn't feel as heavy, especially when the mess up is something out of my control.

Being disconnected and having no emotions are characteristics of a robot. Robots don't have true feelings, they are simply programmed to respond. I walk around with my heart on my sleeve majority of the time. Sometimes as a coping mechanism, during a moment of crisis, I am able to have an out of body experience by ridding myself of any emotions I may have. I pretend I don't even have the ability to respond emotionally. I resort to robot mode until I am able to get past whatever feeling is holding me back. I have the ability to play the emotionless card whenever I feel necessary. I would rather feel nothing at all, than allow myself to get upset about something. As I watch my one year old pull out every single swab and let them lay there all over the floor, I accept the fact that I am able to finish getting ready by letting her do that, and I can look in her direction and turn on my robotics and basically feel nothing at all.

I have previously tried to be in complete control of everything my entire life. I think I am least happy when I try to control everything and everyone. It feels good to me, now, to sometimes not be quite so worried, to be out in the waves in the ocean, floating on top of the water, letting the current take me in whatever direction it wishes. I like the idea of not being able to control something sometimes. Some find the ocean waves and the current terrifying. I know that if I try to be stronger then the current, I will just find myself swimming and swimming, yet going nowhere. So I let it take me and I enjoy the fact that it is out of my control. Yes, I am in charge of my life, of my destiny, but there are things I can't control.

I think my fascination with shows, movies, and books also stems from the idea of not having any control over how the story unfolds. I walk in Barnes and Nobles and automatically I am inhaling that paper smell. Similar to the smell of the post office, when I walk in the book store I am so energized, being surrounded by all these stories. I want to just cram all of them in my brain since I know realistically the amount of time I have to read a book right now with three small children is minimal.

I'll never forget the interview that landed me my teaching position in the county I have been with for the last twelve years. I was asked to tell something that could not be found on my resume. I got dropped jaws with my response that first started out, "I have a superpower." I went on to say how I truly feel like I have this ability to put myself in other people's shoes and feel what they are feeling. This is prevalent when I am invested in a book, movie, or television show. I can empathize with the characters and I feel like more than just a fly on the wall. When they come to a close, I feel... gutted, because I was so invested. I love seeing how other people live and relating to their experiences. I have learned so many life lessons through shows. Queen Charlotte taught me to love others through their flaws and to not judge situations. Firefly Lane helped me to see both sides of the story which helped eliminate the idea of a "bad guy." When we are able to see all perspectives, it's a lot harder to point fingers. Viewing life through third person perspective gives everyone a lot of grace. It gives others grace, but it also allows us to give ourselves grace. We are always hardest on ourselves. I have often taken a step back and told myself, if roles were reversed and I was ideally watching myself, there is no way I would think so horribly of the situation. Movies, shows, books, and literature, helps us find empathy.

Knowing when to turn emotions and feelings on and off is a powerful tool. It is a way to manage and cope through some of the negative situations that could serve as a trigger, and it can help us relate to others before any inaccurate judgment calls are made.

Girl Scouts

Although I haven't been a Brownie for 25 plus years, I still have my vest. The vest holds many badges earned throughout my time as a Girl Scout. These badges do not even come close to the pride I have wearing the badges I have earned over the last few years, the ones that I wear on my invisible vest.

For years, I have worn an invisible Girl Scout vest. And everytime I do something that brings on the feelings of productivity and accomplishment... badge earned! Every single time I wash the bed sheets...badge! All three of my kids are bathed... badge! My husband goes out of town for work for a full week... that's two badges! Vacuum the pool...badge! Play make believe with the kids even though I am exhausted from a full day's work...badge! Go for a run...badge! Do the dishes...badge! Take the laundry up immediately after it is folded...DOUBLE badge! Pack everyone's lunches the night before...badge!

These badges don't require my mom taking my vest to a seamstress, they latch on immediately. They make me feel a sense of pride. And although I may have felt a little pride everytime I earned one when I was seven, at the end of the day, they required very little mental discipline, preparation, agency, convincing, and ownership. NOTHING compared to getting myself to work on time with all I go through each morning...badge! The positive reinforcement I feel from slapping imaginary badges all over my body keeps me energized, motivated, and feeling very accomplished.

Baby Steps

We have all felt like our entire world is caving in on us at some point. This could be due to limited time to complete unsustainable tasks. The best advice I have is taking one baby step at a time, because one baby step gets you a whole lot closer than no steps which usually leads to a mental breakdown. I can often associate this with my workload. Instead of thinking about all the things to do, just focus on one thing. Haven't run in months, don't even try to think about your body in a two piece bathing suit and how much working out it will take to get there, just focus on positivity and maybe run one mile today for the sake of how good it feels when it's under your belt. One mile will invigorate and that little taste will make you want more, and then you can move forward. Get rid of the dress that is too small, obsessing over the idea that you will one day fit back into it. Be happy with your body and your size and stop longing for what you don't have, because as soon as you have it, you will be longing for something else.

Instead of cleaning your whole house, just pick one room to tackle, or set the timer for ten minutes, you'll be amazed at what you can accomplish. Instead of trying to do all the laundry over the weekend, just do one load here and there throughout the week. Just unload the dishwasher instead of refilling it, too. It will be easier to fill the next day if you unload it today. And I read one time to not be afraid of running the dishwasher twice if you don't feel like washing off the dishes before you put them in there. (That won't work for my family because we let them sit too long and the food is too caked on for a dishwasher to remove. I also don't want an electric bill that reflects running that thing twice-- and that can't be good for the environment...but the point was to just do what you have to do, to get by, and don't be ashamed of it).

Lauren Diagle is one of my favorite artists and one of her songs promotes the idea of learning how to be still. Although it seems like an obvious concept, thinking and doing are very different. I can relate to that on so many levels because I have to tell myself to be still if that is my intention. It doesn't come naturally. When I am, I reap the benefits. Walking out from dropping my son off at school, cars that were dropping kids off were roaring past me. For one second, I pretended that swish was the sound of waves and I envisioned myself sitting on the beach, near the ocean. It was calming.

If we could remember the way people treat us is usually a reflection of them, and not us, it will help us to stay patient. Acting and not reacting. I want to be patient with myself and others because I only want to be around people that are patient. I read a quote once that ended with "this moment is the oldest we have ever been, and the youngest we'll ever be again." That gives you all the excuses you need to make the most of the moment. We need to live the dash on our tombstones to the absolute fullest. Andrew Bernstein once said, "Stress doesn't come from what's going on in your life. It comes from your thoughts about what's going on in your life." And I feel Cleo Wade in my veins in the quote, "Don't be the reason someone feels insecure. Be the reason someone feels seen, heard, and supported." We all know people that make us feel insecure. And we all know people that make us feel seen, heard, and supported. I try to stop and ask myself, which one am I if others' perception is all that matters?

Patience

Be patient and look for people who are patient. I search for people that are patient with me. I appreciate my kids when they are patient with me. For example, telling my starving kids to just wait a few more minutes until we got to the birthday party at Ledo's. I got all three of them out, including the baby, and we walked in, and realized there are two Ledo's and I didn't pay attention to the address and we needed to all go get back into car seats and drive farther. I knew they were frustrated but they didn't say anything.

Or when I am rushed to my daughter's doctor's appointment, got there with five minutes to spare, felt very accomplished, and they told me the appointment was made for the Urbana office, instead of the Frederick office. Urbana was about 20 further minutes away. So we got back in the car immediately driving on. I knew she was frustrated with having to get back into her carseat, but she didn't complain. Those behaviors are noted and remind me of the importance of going with the flow and staying calm. Putting us in Urbana however, was a domino effect because I needed to pick my sons up from school. They go to aftercare and don't love it, even though they are perfectly content every time I show up to get them. I work across the street and can get to them within a half hour of their school bell dismissal.

Sometimes it is important to give yourself grace. Adding twenty minutes onto their aftercare stay wasn't going to kill them. Part of me dies inside and feels anxiety and panic as I rush to them leaving the doctors, because I know they say they don't want to be there, while the other, far more sane part of me remembers that they will be okay to stay a few extra minutes on this beautiful autumn day, where they will be playing outside with peers. Telling ourselves that everything "is okay" is a virtue in itself. If you are able to convince yourself that everything is okay in a time of distress, it will most likely make you a far more level headed thinker.

It is important that we are vulnerable, even when it feels embarrassing. I flat out had to tell the insurance lady, retirement 401K guy, and the American Education Student Loans representative, all in the same day, that I had absolutely no idea what they were talking about. In the kindest way possible, I basically had to tell them I need the most dumbed down version of whatever it is they were saying or selling because for some reason when they start talking, they lose me after the first five words. I have never had a poker face, so it is more obvious in person, but over the phone I have to spell out my needed assistance. I figure, I help people everyday as a teacher. If a student doesn't understand a concept, I don't just move on. Companies though will move on, and leave you in the dust, if you are not outspoken, honest, and vulnerable.

Just because I am not an expert in these areas, it is important you find the areas you are. I had just given my daughter a granola bar when the nurse came in to give her shots, at that Urbana office that day. Of course we didn't want anything in her mouth as I lay her down, because she could choke. She was getting upset that the nurse was in there and it was almost as if she was refusing to swallow the food she was chewing because she knew what came next. I knew if I offered her something else she liked, she would spit it out. Babies are so funny, they will spit something out instead of just swallowing it. After three minutes of trying to coax her into spitting it out, I offered her a banana and sure enough, BAM, she spit that sucker out. I looked like I knew exactly what I was doing.

Or when one of my intervention students who has selective mutism at school will only speak to me for a verbal test. Or one of the teachers in your building says you are one of the most inspirational people in their day, and that they have saved every single piece of information you have ever given them in a special drawer in their room. Sometimes we need to give ourselves a little more credit and cling to the things we are good at and accept the things we are not. We need to admire when others are patient with us and be sure to be patient with others.

SOS

I think it is important to remind ourselves
that everyone doesn't want to be saved. That is
such a hard concept to me. Listen to Lauren
Diagle's song SOS. "I will rescue you" are four
words that I can apply to so many situations in my
life that ideally ended up backfiring. I felt
obligated to "send out the troops," because my
personality would have benefited from that
approach if roles were reversed; but just because
that makes me feel good, doesn't mean it makes
everyone else. How do we know when not to
help? Wouldn't you rather be sorry you helped
"too much" than "not enough?" I thought for
sure that would be the better sacrifice, but

multiple times throughout my life I overstepped my boundaries in the other person's eyes.

Just because I approach something one way, does not automatically mean that is how others would appreciate it done. Have you ever heard of everyone having their own "love language?" Life can be so confusing. I have learned we each have our own perspective and although I feel as if what I favor stays predominately the same all the time, it can change with the scenario and the situation. We are better off when we don't ever assume how others would want us to react, and if they are not coming to us, we may need to respect the space they wish to have, and stay in our own lane.

Only One Life

It is sad to me that we only have one life. I want to do everything. I want to be everything and see everything. I love TV shows such as Maid and Bridgerton for the sole fact that it exposes me to different socioeconomic statuses. I know I can give more grace to others if I can find understanding. I wish I could experience different careers and see what life is like being lived in different parts of the world.

My college was in the same town as many Amish families. I would walk dogs at the shelter past their properties and come up with a plan to ask them if I could just stay one night and experience what their life was like first hand. I never had the guts to do it.

I want to be a contestant on so many reality shows I watch like Big Brother (just to see how far I could make it) and Love is Blind (however I really am happily married). I want to be an actor and a nurse. I always wanted to be a bartender.

So how is it that some people can stay at their job, which is in the same building, doing the same exact type of assignment for 30+ years? I don't even like to wear the same outfit twice. Luckily this is my mindset, one that doesn't wish to just "sit still," because it makes me more resilient when it comes to dodging obstacles. When I earned my Master's from a college that was promoted by my current employer (literally they advertised for the university hosting a meal to all those prospective students at a fancy restaurant that were interested in hearing their pitch), had my entire degree paid for by my employer, took SEVEN years to obtain the degree due to coaching a high school varsity lacrosse team and then having babies, and was granted a position as a Literacy Specialist, which requires this degree, I was never once shown a single red flag regarding not having the proper credentials or qualifications. After being in the role for three full years, I was all of a sudden told by my administrator, director, and Human Resources that I did not have the required degree to be in my position due to the degree I had was not from an "accredited" or "licensed" institution. After I had mentored graduate students who earned their Literacy Specialist degree, completed a one year practicum on a Dyslexia intervention training, led my county in piloting a blended learning approach to education, became LETRS certified, etc. all of a sudden I am going to be ripped from my role because somehow I got a job that I wasn't qualified for? Didn't then and doesn't now seem quite right. BUT guess what, I didn't want to be locked into a specific role (besides being a mother) my whole life, because I want to be everything. And this just might be the nudge I need to go out and see what else is out there. I may have cried for five minutes about it, but I didn't let it ruin my life.

I don't see how people can live in the same house their whole lives and never modernize or update/renovate it. How can women wear their hair the same exact way every single day their entire life without getting bored with it? But I will accept and celebrate that everyone is different and if we were all the same, the world would be a nightmare. I hate that life feels so short. I can't stand the fact that it is not reasonable to obtain multiple degrees, providing the opportunity for multiple careers. I am grateful for the optimism I wake up with in the morning to seize the day and try and find all there is to see, even if that comes from someone else making a decision for me that rips me from where I have had roots growing for quite some time.

Right before I got pregnant with my third child, my husband and I watched some documentaries on cutting out meat from our diets. The documentaries didn't have anything to do with animal rights, but more so the health benefit of eliminating meat. Sure I wanted to give it a try, because, why not? I went strong for a couple weeks, before I found out I was pregnant. Before the McDonald's Big Mac cravings began. I always wanted a Big Mac and there was no stopping me. My husband thought for sure I would jump back on the bandwagon with him once my sweet baby girl was out. Not a chance.

If I only get one life and I LOVE steak, I am not cutting it out of my diet. So my husband compromised and simply leaves RED meat out of his diet. Well, turkey burgers have nothing on real burgers, but what am I supposed to do, cook two different meals?! Freaking turkey. Out of slight resentment, I am reading *The F*ck it Diet* by

Caroline Dooner, which so far pretty much sums up my thoughts on getting rid of anything else I love to eat.

7 Crowns, 1 Tooth Extraction, 3 Cavity Fillings

I definitely know it could be worse, but I also know I have brushed my six year old's teeth every single morning and night basically since he had teeth. I will be completely honest, I do not brush my own teeth before I go to bed at night because I wasn't raised that way. And my teeth were fine. But damn do my kids' teeth get brushed religiously. And my six year old who chooses water over other drinks and likes chocolate way more than any gummy candy, just went under at a hospital in Baltimore to get seven crowns put on his teeth, along with a tooth extraction (cracked molar), and three filings done.

The nurse asked him at the hospital if he wore pull-ups, (he's six) because he needed to put one on while he was "asleep." He looked at me and we were both mortified. He was mortified at the thought of putting on a diaper and I was mortified that this nurse would be asking a six year old if he currently wore diapers. He had Tylenol administered through his rear end and an IV. He had very few teeth not touched during this procedure. And I can't help but think to myself, HOW IS THIS HAPPENING? How is it that I can't remember any of my childhood friends having golden teeth, but when I am at school, I am surrounded by kids that have extracted teeth and crowns? Kids that are struggling to learn phonics because they don't have teeth in place to help make the sounds, or phonemes. They have holes that last for years because the adult tooth under it is nowhere near ready to surface.

At first, the dentist told us he would need these front tooth fillings and there was a chance his teeth would fall out during the process. Well, this already was a sore subject for my son because he was in first grade and still hadn't had a wiggly tooth. All of his friends were losing teeth and he was so upset every time he heard someone else's fell out. My kids got their teeth late in the game to begin with, and if it is hereditary, I didn't lose my first tooth until second grade. There was no way he was going to wake up from this procedure with missing teeth, when he didn't even get to experience this milestone yet. This is my sweet boy that threw up walking into school on his first day because of anxiety, and not to mention it was in the middle of the COVID pandemic when most schools were shut down, and ours was still going strong. (We got so many nasty looks that morning, there was no way I would be able to convince the school he wasn't sick, and that it was just anxiety. These were the COVID times of temperatures being checked before walking into the building every single day.)

Sometimes I wish I had something like a "Mom Rule Book" because I didn't even know I had the right to tell the dentist she wasn't going to remove those front teeth. But after asking multiple people I confided in, we scheduled another appointment right before the surgery and the dentist assured me they wouldn't fall out due to not being even remotely loose.

We switched dentists a while ago. We went through nightmare after nightmare. My four year old was told he needed five fillings after a previous appointment six months earlier where I was told his teeth looked perfect. So I went for a second opinion, walking in thinking the verdict would be so much better and my walk out would be full of positive news, only to be patted on the back by the chauvinist dentist that said, "I see twelve cavities that will need filled, mom." He literally patted me on the back while saying this. A pediatric dentist, or should I say a heartless fool that had no care in the world for my son or me that day.

We had a family friend that was a dental hygienist for 40 plus years. I asked her to look in his mouth and she recommended doing nothing due to how nice his teeth looked. So three completely opposite directions I was being pulled in, and not over something little... over my child, who was already terrified of the dentist. So although it takes us 45 minutes to get there, we now drive to a dentist we love and trust. A dentist that we don't feel is trying to meet a monthly quota for the number of filled cavities.

What a horrifying thought, especially when I am not a dentist. I always worried about people that take care of things of mine, that I really know nothing about. For instance, you take your car into the shop, and they tell you you need all this work done, when in reality, you don't know if they are just keeping themselves in business. You have no way of knowing if what they are saying is legitimate. You just have to accept it and pay hundreds or thousands of dollars.

So after finally finding a conservative dentist we trusted, we followed through with the procedure they were saying he so badly needed. My son made it through his dental surgery. I was worried he would wake up from his anesthesia the same way he came out of it from his eye surgery he had the year before. Thinking back to that eye surgery, I was super pregnant. Only one parent was allowed and it was a huge debate with my husband because he so badly wanted to be the one. But at the end of the day, I gave birth to the child, and so that trumps everything. I won. My emotions were wild during my third trimester so when the secretary said I couldn't go back because I was pregnant, before we even made it inside the triage, my crying must have been the only reason she let me go. Uncontrollable tears are something I will never miss from the pregnancy hormones. Not a good look for my son who was probably terrified already inside. No one told us he could wake up from anesthesia raging. I am only familiar with those that wake up from wisdom teeth removal and always appear drunk, lethargic, and silly. Not my child, he woke up raging, kicking, punching, trying to pull his IV out, and rip off his eye dressing. I hid my very pregnant belly behind the bed railing to save it from a severe blow. It worked!

So my worst fear was living through this again. The nightmare was not relived because he woke up much calmer. But these are the things I could have prepared myself for, had I known, but instead had to find out the hard way. They also thought he would be willing to go from the triage to the surgery area without me. A pediatric eye doctor thought a six year old would just graciously leave their mother and stroll on back with them. Why is it that sometimes people just need shook, or in other words, brought back to reality. So we basically had to drug him until he was willing to go back without me. I was crying and he was crying. What a scene!

I later found out, had I gone with my son prior to the surgery to his pediatrician and gotten a proper anxiety diagnosis (which could have been so easily proven), I would have been able to go back THE WHOLE WAY with him.

Sometimes it doesn't matter, even if you think you are doing everything right. I didn't know that our brand of mouthwash countered the prescription toothpaste, so they canceled each other out, making neither effective. I didn't know flossing after we brushed teeth was an issue, or that using one of the single thread flossers almost defeated the entire purpose of flossing your teeth (because the same part of the dental floss continuously goes in and out, dirtying other teeth that might not have been dirty in the first place).

Sometimes we get lost in the life we thought we were "supposed to have," forgetting "what we have" is what was made for us. And sometimes, we would do anything to switch places with our children to tag them out of whatever hardships they must go through. And sometimes, even after doing everything right, we still blame ourselves. And that is okay, because we are human.

Mario Party

You know the memories or feelings that get dug up, out of the grave, after being exposed to some sensory experience associated with a past time? Memories you don't even remember you were holding onto until something so quickly takes you back. Something as simple as a car smell (more specifically Black Ice) from an old RAM truck. Or buying a cheap ladies deodorant that takes you back to high school sports, or an Herbal Essences Body Envy Volumizing Hairspray with Citrus Essences, that takes you back to your college dorm room.

I know that in order to remember moments vividly enough to physically and mentally feel like I am back in old shoes, from many years ago, shows I had to have really lived through those moments the first time around. I am pretty sensory oriented, and I think my middle son got his texture sensory issues possibly from me, if that is even something hereditary. No, I never insisted on wearing skin tight pajamas to bed as a child, or at least that I can remember, but I do know I lead with my senses.

I get frustrated seeing my husband drink a milkshake so fast or eat his dinner in what seems like one bite, because I like to taste it. Phones have thrown a whole new twist on wanting to experience life first hand, because many people are seeing it second hand, videoing life's moments behind the screen of their phone. They are more worried about watching it behind their camera so the moment is captured, but is the moment really captured if it was never fully experienced or felt? I too want to have everything recorded or stored for later, but how much of life are we missing, worrying so much about how much we can ideally save for "later?"

My thoughts started for this chapter as I sit playing Mario Party on Nintendo Switch with my two sons. It was a childhood FAVORITE of mine. I would go to one of my best friends' houses and we would sit there and just play it for hours. I don't know why my admiration for the game was so high, as I sat there today trying to figure it out. Thinking about what life looked like when I was seven, having all the time in the world, to just sit beside a best friend in her guest bedroom and just play video games. With no sense of time or worry over whatever I was doing and how it was keeping me away from what I really should be doing instead. I worry that sometimes I do take life for granted. I am sad that we sometimes never truly know the value of a moment until it is in the past.

As I sat there with my sons today I remembered the sound of those coins as Princess

Peach collected three from landing on another gameboard spot. I can remember the skill it took to win the "Tug-of-War" rope mini game by swirling your palm around the little rotating button. I can feel the increase in dopamine as I collected a star on the board, putting me into the ever changing, first place.

Sometimes, with all the chaos happening around us, we forget to take in the little moments that will bring us back to that very second years and years later.

Morning Routine

It is amazing how much power the first couple minutes of your day can control. They are the hardest and require the most self discipline because they are required when you are at your weakest, when you are just waking up, feeling so comfortable and vulnerable and unmotivated because of the state of tranquility you may be in. But it is those moments that can set your day up for complete success.

My routine, if followed through, would look like this... working out with the Peloton. Drinking water throughout the workout and after. Getting a shower, shaving my legs, grabbing the lunch that was packed the night before (and not in the morning). Every child where they need to be for the day (both boys at school, the baby with her GiGi or Gram). Walking into my office at work and turning on my essential oils diffuser and all three of my lights (one lamp that was in my husband's house when he was little, a faux tree-- which when I bought it didn't know that faux meant fake, but instead thought it was a type of tree, *that then leads me down the rabbit hole of remembering when I refused to order spinach dip from the menu because I thought artichoke hearts were some type of animal hearts*, with christmas lights all over it, and the rainbow light my son gave me for Christmas this year). If I can make it through those steps -- and in a dream world, would also include making my bed, which has never been a priority but I always wish it was, because I know the feeling of getting into a made bed as the housekeeper does it every other Thursday, I know my day is going to be great. I set myself up for success because I put in the small amounts of time doing that preparation work. I think of it like a court case. A lawyer doesn't just walk into a case and start presenting and it goes well. They have to do their research and come in with all the behind the scenes work completed, but invisible.

So when you're faced with morning surprises like when my daughter rips off her diaper and poops in multiple spots all over the floor. And as I am cleaning one spot, the dog is eating the other spots. Then throws up. It's because I had a workout in and can face the situation with a laugh instead of a cry because my mindset is clear. Or, since now I am thinking about poop, when you are in the above ground pool at your house with four kids you are watching and my son says he needs to poop and you don't want to make everyone get out of the pool (so I can go inside and help him wipe) you feel confident talking up a dog's lifestyle of being able to poop in the yard and convince that son to follow suit.

Every scenario thrown at you, during your day, will subconsciously be dealt with based on your mindset, that was most likely put in place the first couple minutes of your day. Don't cheat yourself out of the work. Don't settle for less. Don't doubt yourself and never permanently quit (you can temporarily quit, but don't permanently quit).

You can test your mindset by the feelings you have when you wake up to a rainy day. Can you find peace in hearing the rhythmic drops gravity is causing to pitter patter down from the sky, onto the pavement, and gratitude in knowing you are somewhere dry? Or does it ruin your day before it even begins? Do you just "get wet"?

Sometimes it doesn't matter that you do everything right, or how early you leave the house in the morning, because you have no control over that recycling truck or school bus you are forced to sit patiently behind. Find peace in the moments you have no control over, such as the dark indoor water tube slide you fly down like a torpedo at Hershey Lodge. Allow the weight to be taken off your shoulders as you engage in moments that can't be even altered by your efforts.

Admitting life is "a lot" is one of the most powerful statements. I used to think brave people never showed weakness, but I have quickly learned when weakness is labeled and identified and brought to the light, it is never as heavy as when it was in hiding. Asking for help is something the smartest and strongest people do. And until we manage our load by leaning on others, we will put forth so much more effort than necessary.

"Don't regret the moment, own the moment," Peloton instructor Robin Arzon says, a message she leaves her followers at the end of every workout. And just remember every stage of this life is a phase, it's temporary. We are never stuck, even when we convince our brains we are.

Both of my sons have different levels of anxiety. My middle son has separation anxiety and although my intentions were purely signing him up for a three hour basketball camp for one week this summer, I quickly realized, although his brother was there with him, there was no way I was dropping him off and leaving by myself. I was either going to stay for three hours or he would be leaving with me upon arrival. So I stayed. For three hours, with a two year old, for five days in a row, in a confined space in the gymnasium. I was the only parent to stay out of probably forty-five or more kids. But that is motherhood to me. I decided I would own the moment instead of regretting it. I packed all kinds of things for my two year old to do. I figured, we would just be going home to play so we might as well play here. We did play-doh, and books, candy, snacks, dry erase board, and baby dolls. I was able to watch the boys play and to be honest, I don't know if I could have felt the pride I had for them out there if I wasn't there to see it. Others weren't behaving and maybe they would have been if their mom was sitting and watching, but my boys were top of the line. They are little for such a high hoop and large basketball, but they never stopped trying.

I read a really great poem once, written by someone I didn't know but felt like they understood me. It was about the idea of it not being "my turn yet" because right now my priority is being a mom. It will be my turn one day, once my kids get a little older, to go out and do more things for myself. The thought helps me not get wrapped up in my friends' lives when they are out doing destination getaways with their husbands or taking girl trips across the country to sit in hot springs (which I have really always wanted to do...). I've learned everyone's amount of needed self care is different. One of my good friends just got back from a trip to New Zealand where she ventured by herself for two weeks. My self care mostly consists of making sure I take my make-up off at night. Her self care and mine are quite different. And that is okay because my turn will come.

I am that mom that can find self care in slipping out to the grocery store by myself. Getting a margarita from the Mexican Restaurant beside Food Lion, to go, so I have it while shopping. Okay, I never actually did that, but I have dreamed of it. It sure would help the $350 grocery bill not cut so deep.

I can remember leaving the grocery store one evening, after ordering a pizza to be picked up on my way home, to have for dinner that night with my family. I ate a piece in the parking lot because I knew the second I got in the door, I would not stand a chance.

I walked in pretending to be upset, showing my husband what the pizza looked like when I opened it up, with a missing piece. Out of concern he picked up his phone ready to call in (I totally got him). Self care for me is allowing myself to eat the piece of pizza in the car before walking in the door sometimes.

I find it hard to devote time to self care because I grew up with a mom that didn't ever seem to need it. I never saw her do anything for herself, really. So my brain goes there when I want to do something for me. But everyone is different and everyone needs different things and because we know that, we shouldn't judge each other. We should support each other.

I think it is important to know that kids don't know an adult's intentions, they only know what they see the adult do. So the intentions behind taking the kids to a playground won't be what they remember, more so their person sitting there on their phone the entire time. That is what they see, so that is what they will remember. They will remember the undivided attention that was given to them while at the park, even if it is just sitting and watching them play or better yet, going down the slide with them. That in itself is stressful because our phones play so many roles in our lives these days. They are our camera, connection to the outside world, our bank account, and email-- but our kids don't know any of that yet. They just see something that is winning over the attention of their parents.

Find the friends that want the best for you. The friends that make the suggestions you so blatantly missed, that make your life that much better. We were at Dave and Buster's one time and my one year old insisted on putting the debit-like-looking-game-card that you load money onto, to play the games, into the slots, with no intention of riding the ride or playing the game. After taking it from her and seeing her fall apart each time, one of my best friends suggested getting a blank one from the front so she could do her thing, without hindering the points of her brothers for whom the original card belonged to. It is moments like that where I am reminded of how much sweeter life is surrounded by people that have your best interest at heart. And if you don't have anyone like that, they are out there. Once you find them, hold them so tight.

Find what makes you thrive. Because life is worth so much more than just trying and surviving. I think back to Mandy Moore's role in the classic, *A Walk to Remember* and how she is notorious for not letting what anyone else thought of her affect her. Although it may have taken her Leukemia diagnosis to get her mindset to that point, I don't know that we need a diagnosis. A lot of times considering how others perceive us holds us back from living our best life. Our happiness will come when we find confidence in who we are, because "everyone else" IS already taken. To just conform is a way of falling through the cracks, not so much a medal worthy honor. A prayer I made up, that I say with my son each night before he falls asleep goes like this, "Please dear God, help to make me the **best that I** can be, and **thank you** for making me, me."

I wish you the self discipline to always follow your heart as you become the "best you," whether it is as a friend, a parent, a sibling, a coach, mentor, or a neighbor.

You totally got this.

If this book held your attention, look for *Still Trying, Still Surviving. Still Thriving* coming out December of 2023.

Made in the USA
Middletown, DE
26 September 2023

38955703R00076